Little Zoi

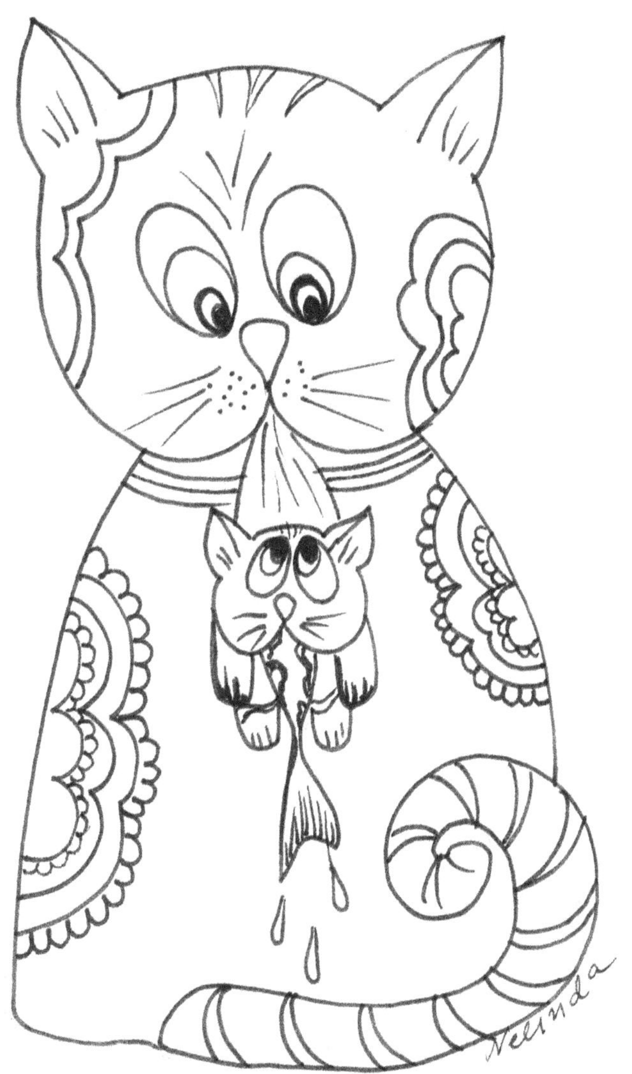

coloring book by Ronesa Aveela- illustrated by Nelinda

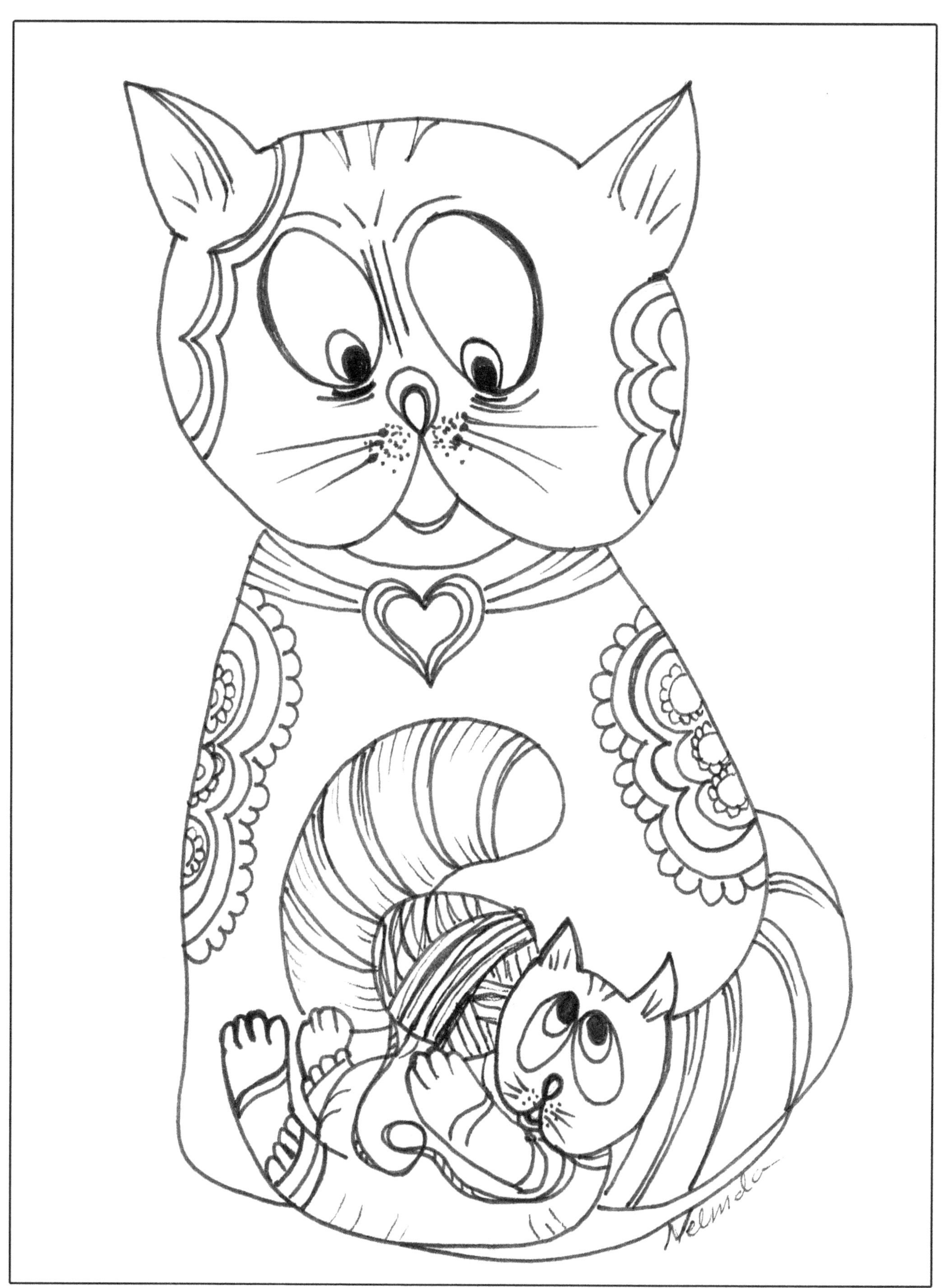

www.ronesaaveela.com

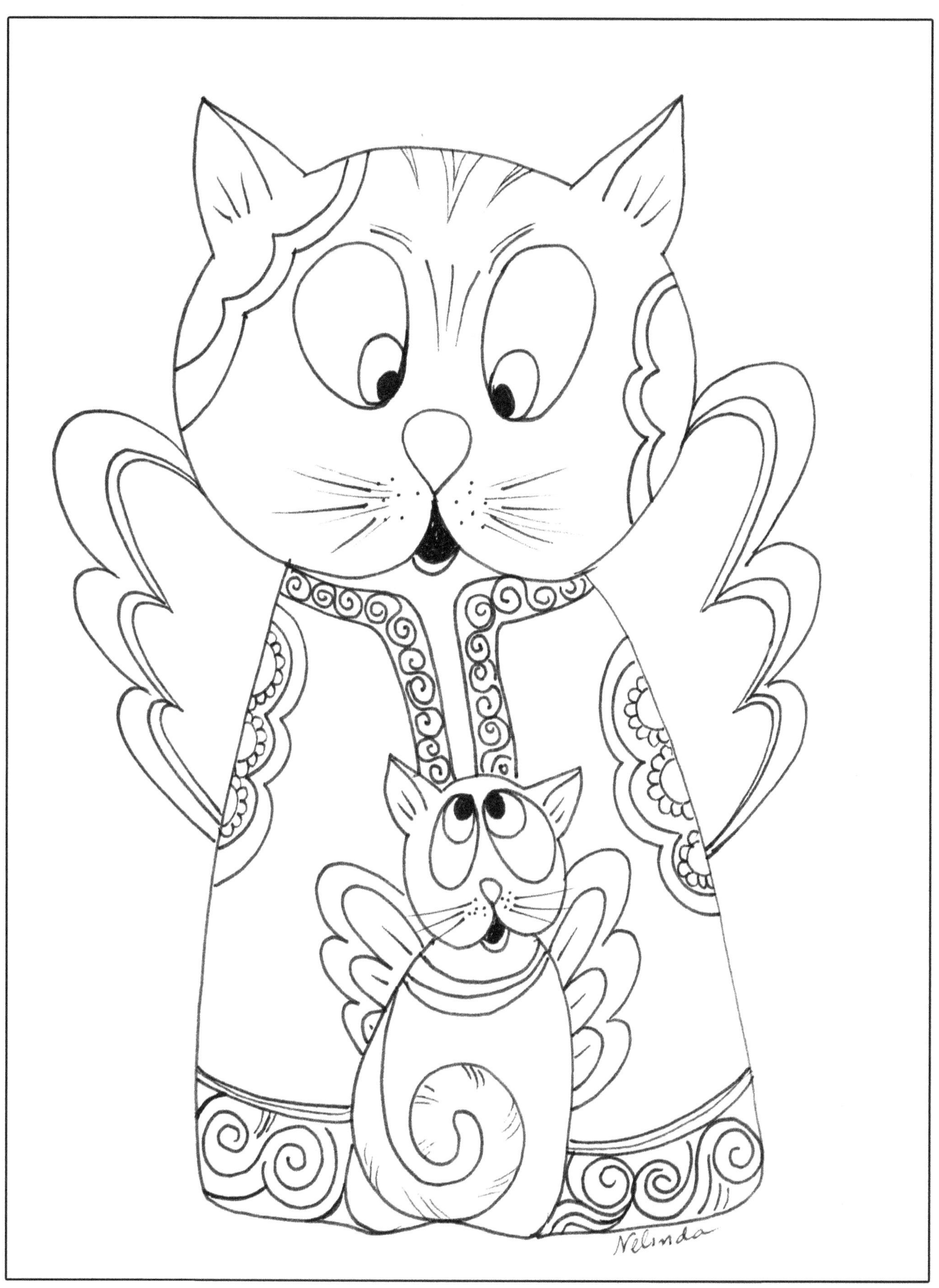

www.ronesaaveela.com

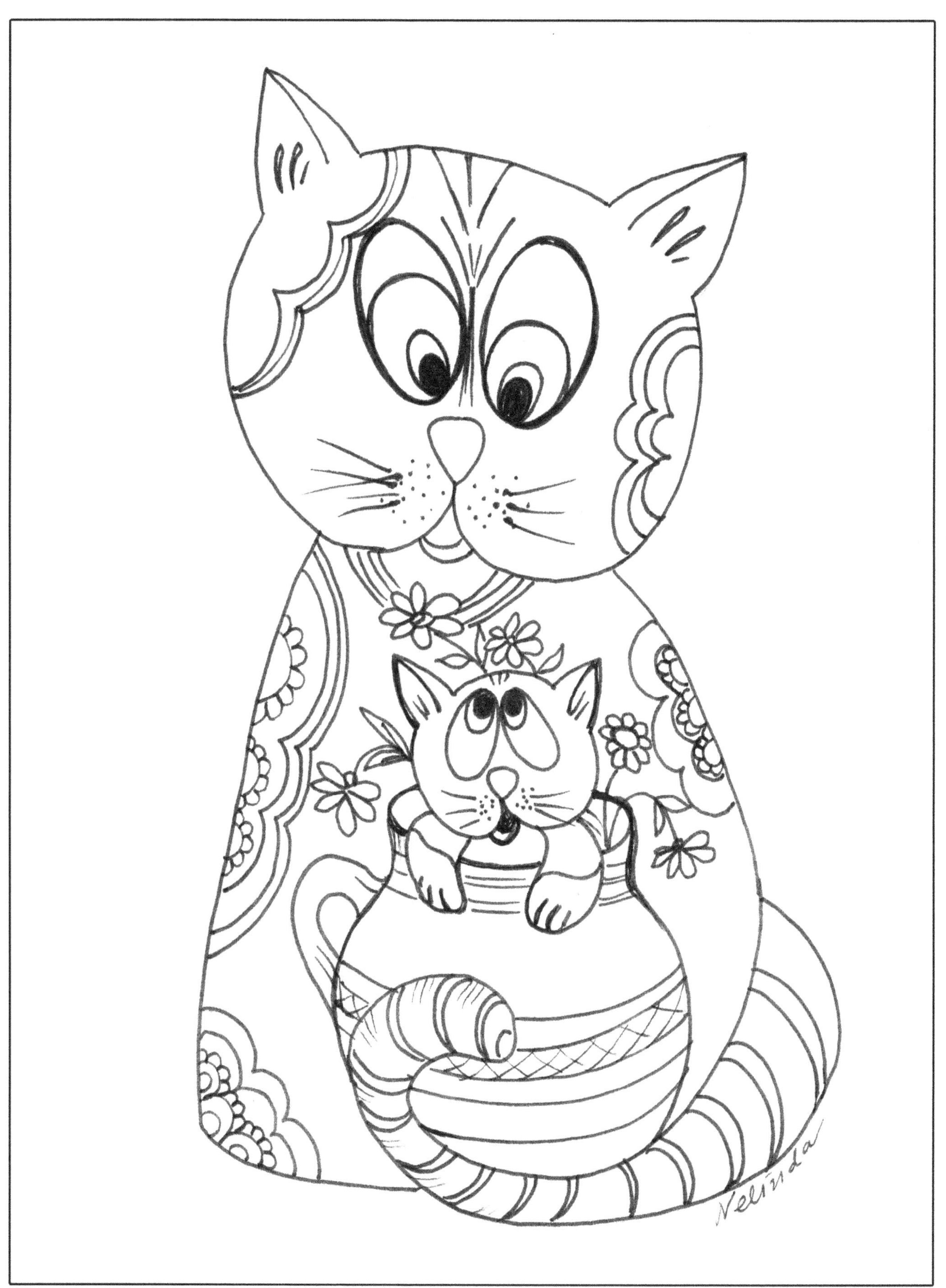

www.ronesaaveela.com

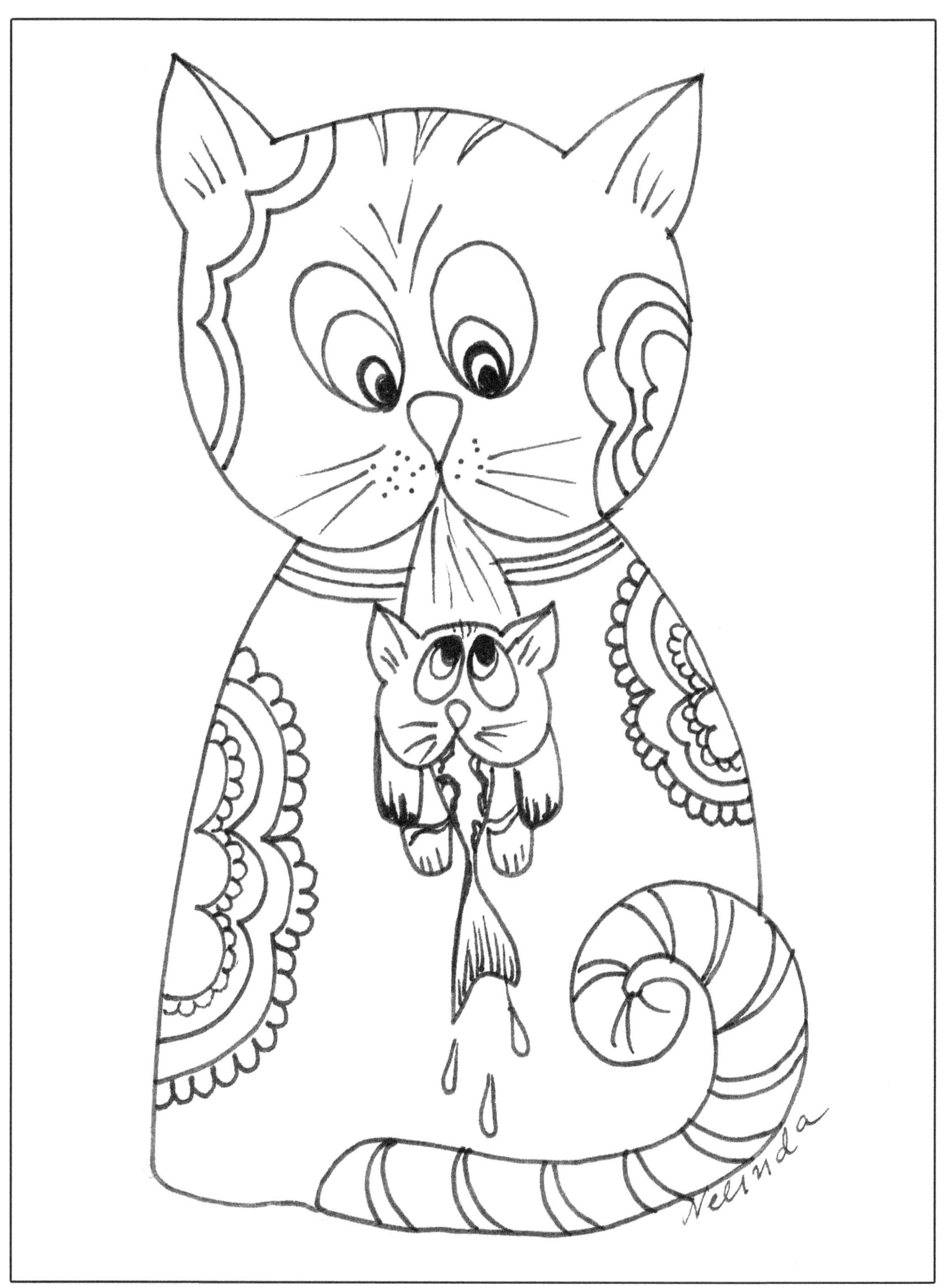

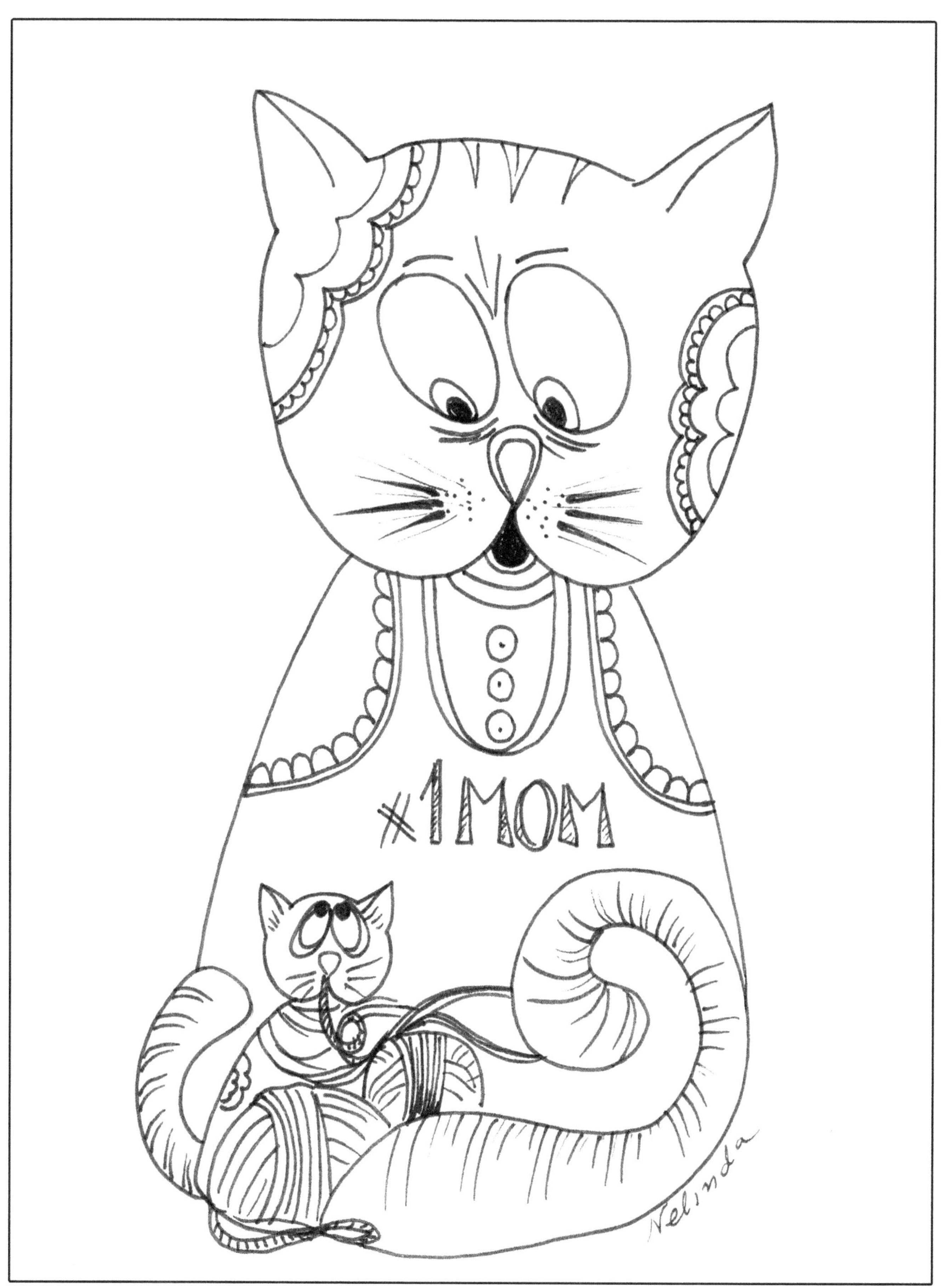

#1MOM
Nelinda

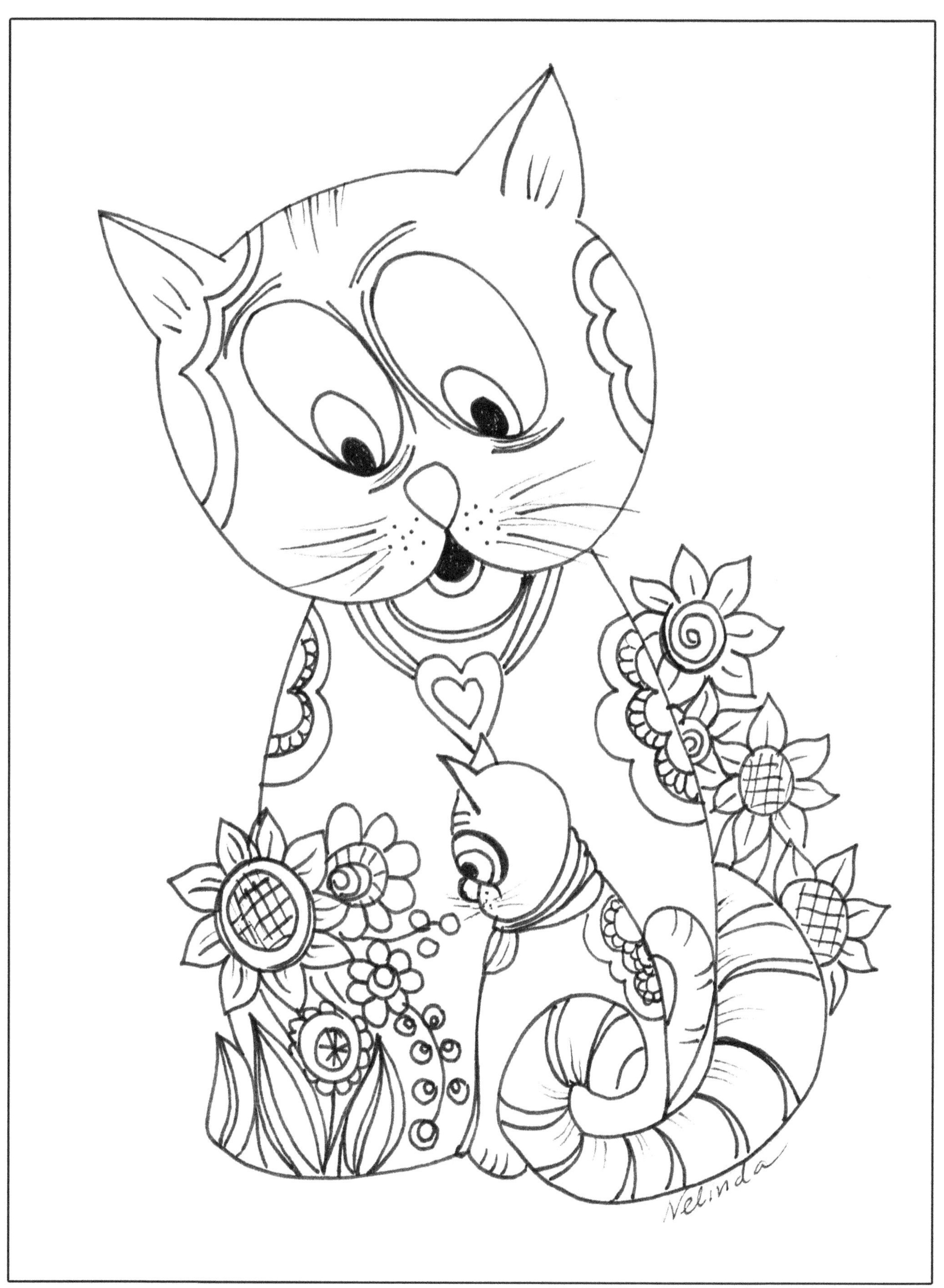

www.ronesaaveela.com

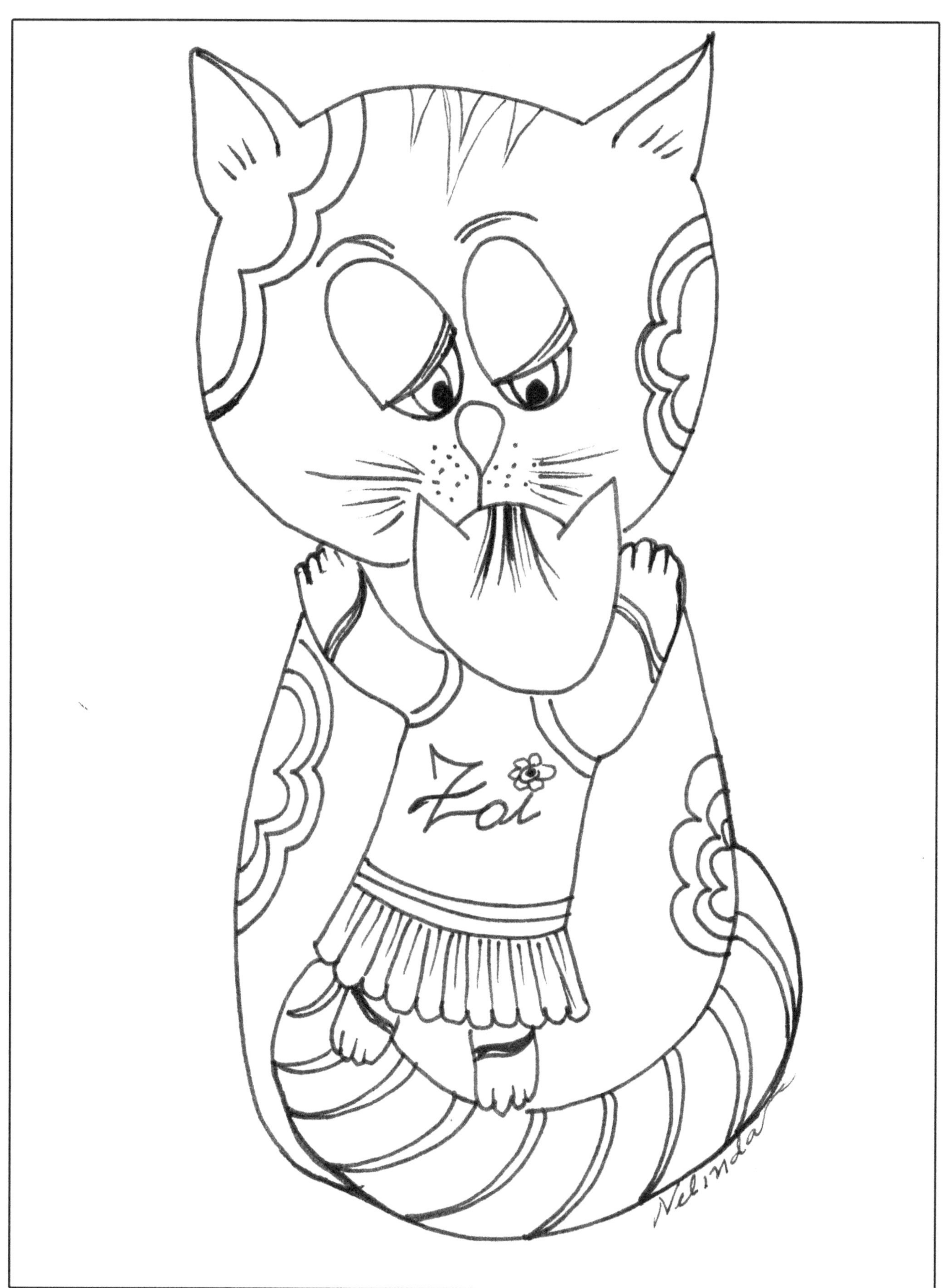

www.ronesaaveela.com

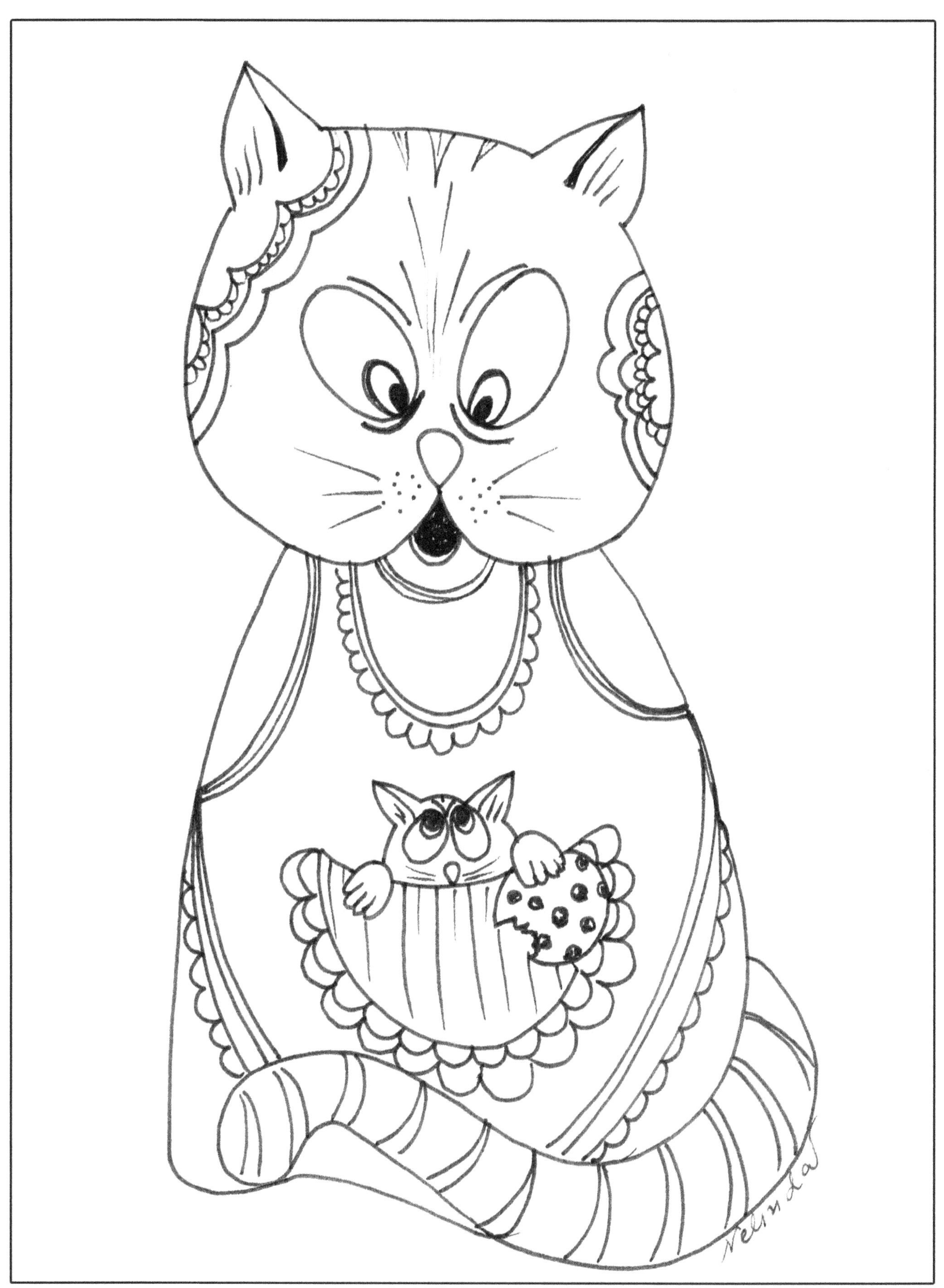

www.ronesaaveela.com

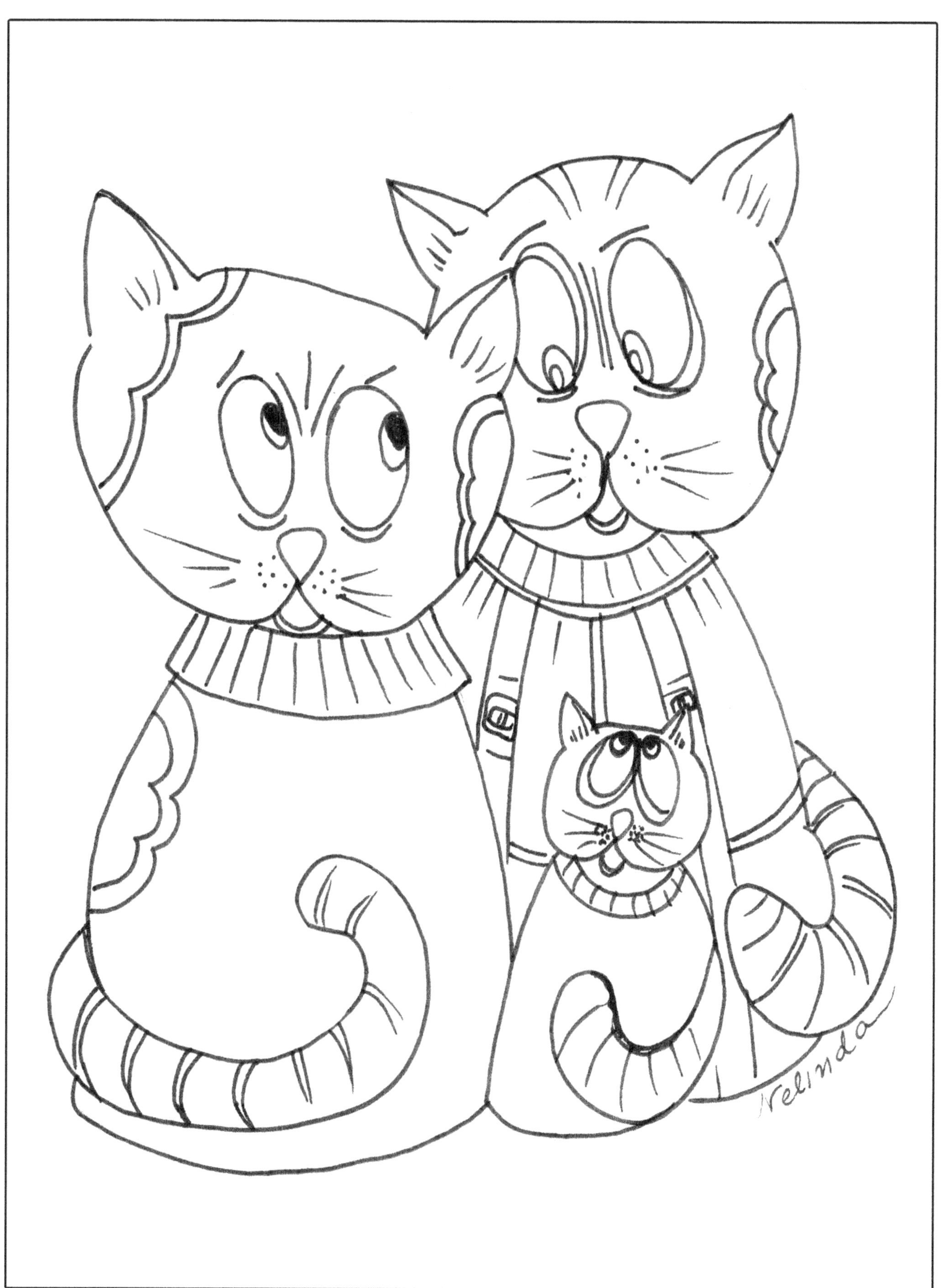

www.ronesaaveela.com

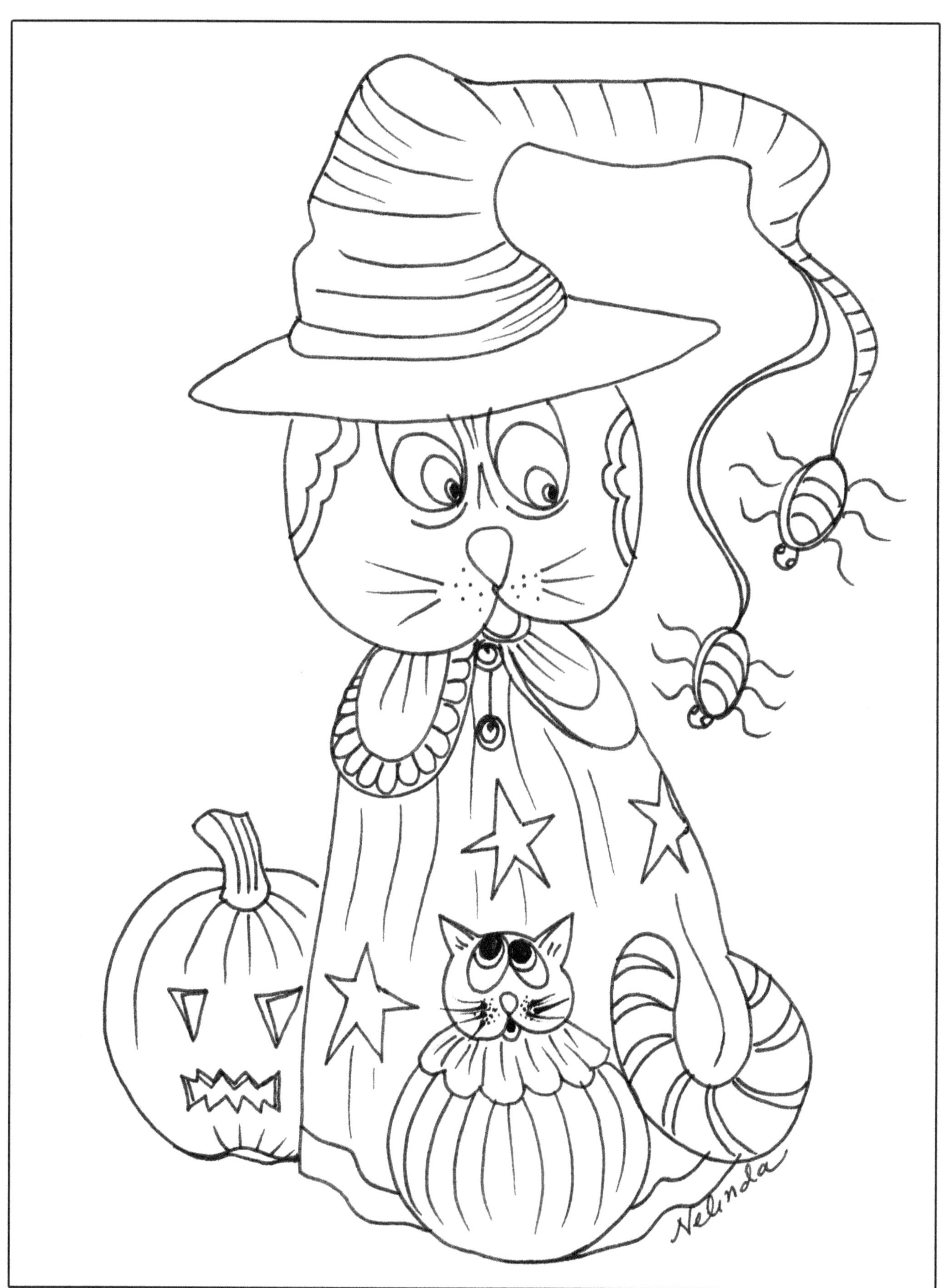

www.ronesaaveela.com

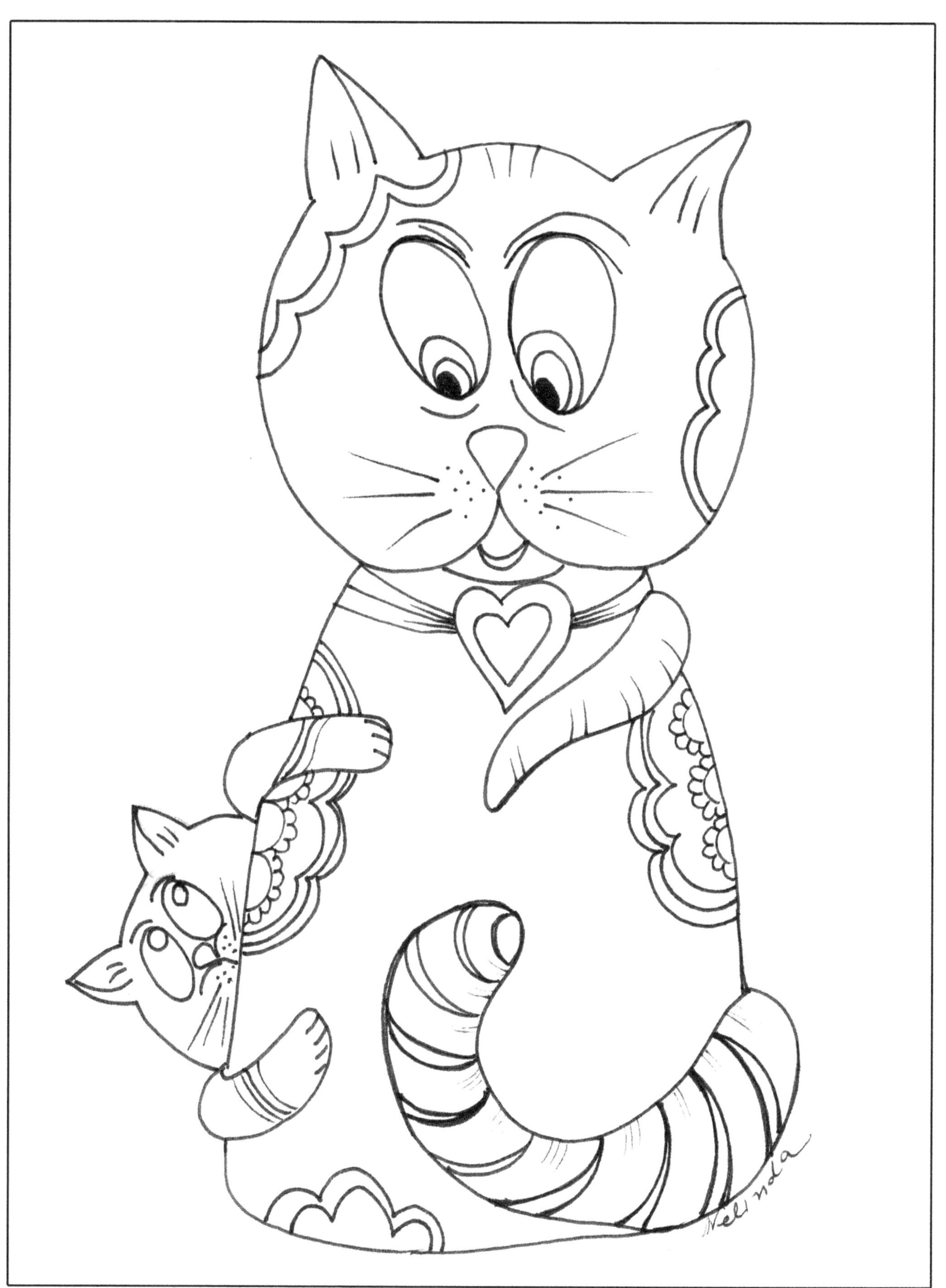

www.ronesaaveela.com

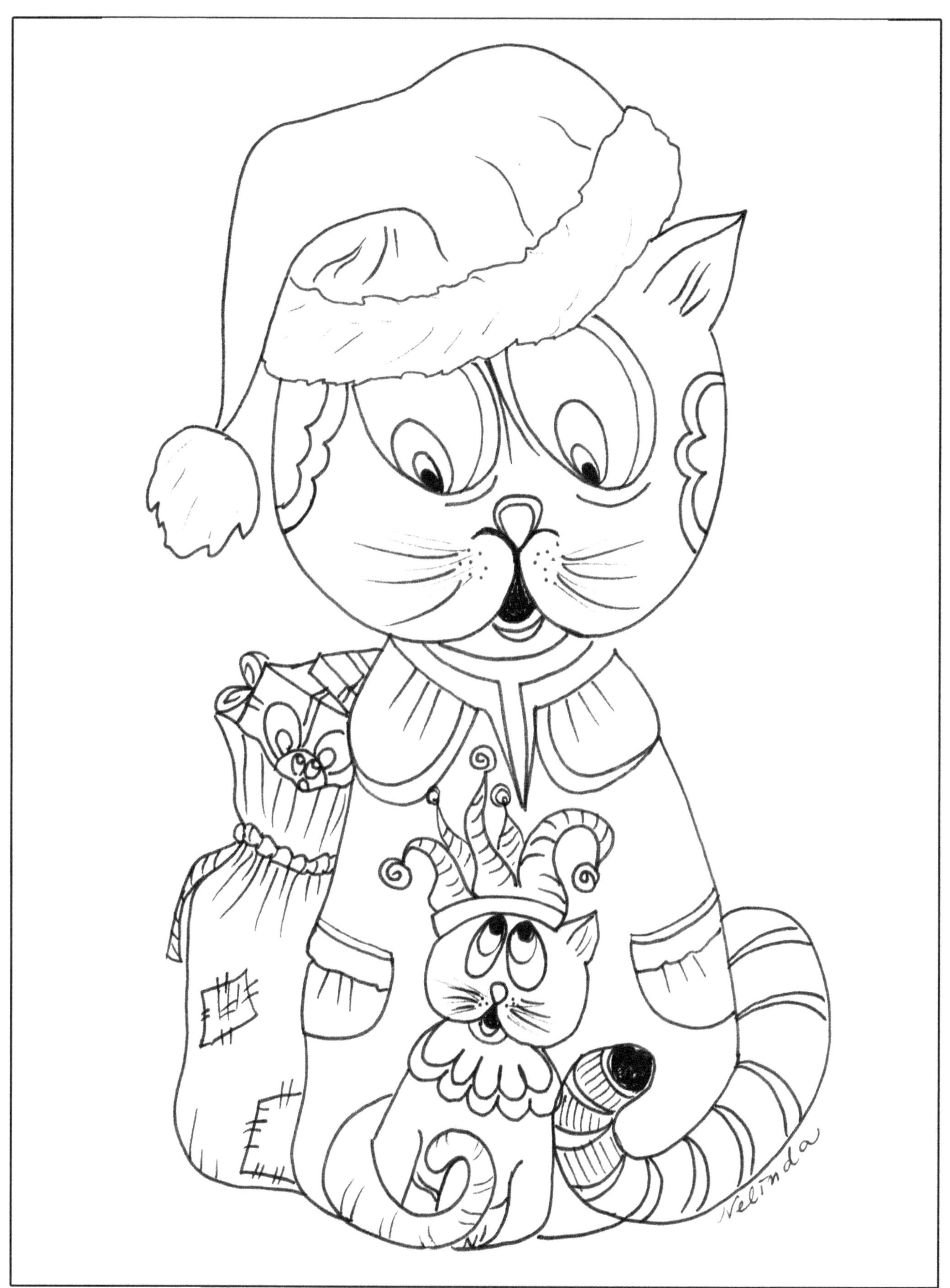

www.ronesaaveela.com

About the Author

Ronesa Aveela is "the creative power of two." Nelly, the main force behind the work, the creative genius, was born in Bulgaria and moved to the U.S. in the 1990s. She grew up with stories of wild Samodivi, Kikimora, the dragons Zmey and Lamia, Baba Yaga, and much more. She's a freelance artist and writer. She likes writing mystery romance inspired by legends and tales. In her free time, she paints. She is married and has two children.

Rebecca, her writing partner, was born and raised in the New England area. She has a background in writing and editing, as well as having a love of all things from different cultures. She's learned so much about Bulgarian culture, folklore, and rituals, and writes to share that knowledge with others.

Connect with us at www.ronesaaveela.com!

www.ingramcontent.com/pod-product-compliance
Lightning Source LLC
Chambersburg PA
CBHW080322030726
47593CB00009B/2852